This Book Belongs To

Beth Williams

given To her
By Her mother, Lynne
Valentine's Day '89

LOVE POTIONS

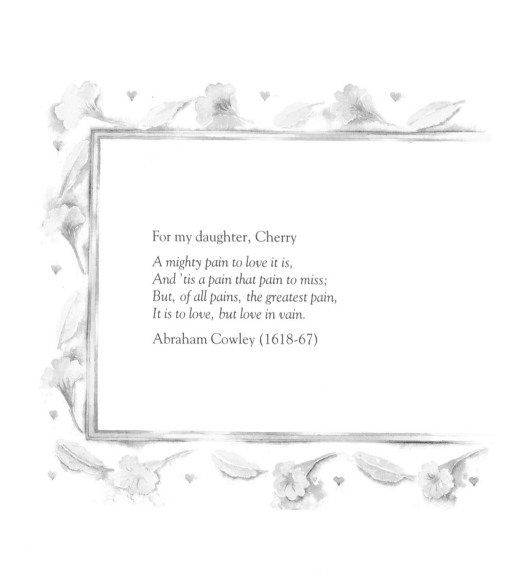

For my daughter, Cherry

A mighty pain to love it is,
And 'tis a pain that pain to miss;
But, of all pains, the greatest pain,
It is to love, but love in vain.

Abraham Cowley (1618-67)

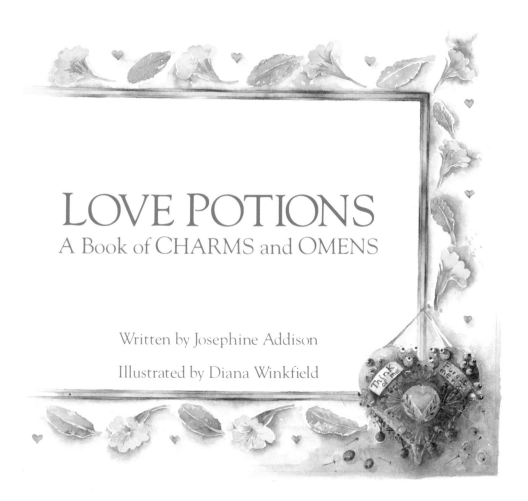

LOVE POTIONS
A Book of CHARMS and OMENS

Written by Josephine Addison

Illustrated by Diana Winkfield

Salem House Publishers

Topsfield, Massachusetts

First published in the United States by
Salem House Publishers,
462 Boston Street,
Topsfield,
MA 01983

Editors: Annabel Edwards and Libby Joy
Designers: Leslie & Lorraine Gerry

Library of Congress Cataloging-in-Publication Data
Addison, Josephine, 1930—
    Love potions, charms, and omens.
    Includes index.
    1. Aphrodisiacs.   2. Charms.   3. Omens.
4. Folklore—Great Britain.   5. Great Britain—Social
life and customs.   I. Title.
GR460.A33 1987   398'.352   87-4725
ISBN 0-88162-240-0

ISBN 0 88162 240 0

Printed in Singapore

CONTENTS

PREFACE

This book of charms and omens is a glance at the many aspects of that delightful problem – falling in love. It makes use of the whole natural world, from flowers, birds, insects and animals to the planets and stars; objects as familiar to our ancestors as they are to us.

Many of the symbols and signs in this book have their roots firmly planted in the mythology of the ancient Greeks and Romans, in the days when every flower was an emblem of a god, and every tree the abode of a nymph. Then the groves surrounding temples were as sacred as the temples themselves and there are many stories of lovers changed into trees and flowers.

With the coming of Christianity, those flowers and trees were assigned to saints, and churches were often built on pagan sites. Inevitably the festivals and customs of the different traditions became interwoven. The love divination ceremonies, and the charms that evolved from them gave stability to young lives often shrouded in fear and superstition. A question asked at one particular time of year was answered by the changing face of nature as the year unfolded, including the special days and months of the year when an engagement or wedding should take place. Of course, the customs and origins of St. Valentine's Day have a special place in the lover's calendar.

A fine web of superstition still patterns our lives, as we almost unconsciously throw salt over our shoulders, touch wood, cross our fingers, avoid ladders and pick petals off a daisy, saying 'He loves me, he loves me not.' We are not, I am delighted to say, so very different from our ancestors.

LOVE POTIONS

CYCLAMEN symbolizes diffidence and voluptuousness, but our ancestors used the plant as an aphrodisiac, believing that if eaten it induced one to fall in love.

HERB PARIS possesses narcotic properties and was regarded generally as a powerful ingredient for love philtres. The herb was probably dedicated to Paris, symbol of perfect manhood, whose love for Helen made their story one of the most famous in history.

LETTUCE is said to be an aphrodisiac, and a soup made from the powdered genitalia of a timid bull, mixed with lettuce and purslane, is a powerful one. In Greek mythology, Venus laid the body of her lover on a bed of lettuce, while Juno, wife of Jupiter, conceived Hebe after eating lettuce.

Many parents forbade their teenage daughters to bring the fragrant HONEYSUCKLE into the house as it was thought to induce erotic dreams. However, another custom says that if honeysuckle is brought indoors a wedding will follow shortly.

In legend Cupid shot an arrow at the WILD PANSY, sometimes known as heartsease or love-in-idleness. Originally white, the wound caused it to change colour, and the juice of the plant was used as a love potion, as Oberon explains in William Shakespeare's *Midsummer Night's Dream:*

Yet marked I where the bolt of cupid fell,
It fell upon a little Western flower.
Before, milk-white, now purple with love's wound;
The maidens call it Love-in-idleness.
Fetch me that flower; the herb I showed thee once;
The juice of it on sleeping eye-lids laid,
Will make man or woman madly dote,
Upon the next live creature that it sees.

The PERIWINKLE enjoyed a considerable reputation as an aphrodisiac, and even Culpeper advised that the leaves eaten together 'by a man and

wife cause love between them'. A less savoury love potion, used in the same way, consists of powdered periwinkle, houseleek, and earthworms.

QUINCE symbolizes love, fruitfulness and temptation and the ancient Greeks and Romans held it in great honour. The fruit was sacred to Venus, and newly-married couples traditionally shared the fruit as a symbol of their love. A passage from *In Praise of Musicke,* published in 1586, states the 'eating of a Quince Peare to be preparative of sweet and delightful days between married persons'. Dream of the quince, and you will be successful in love.

The dainty, pale lilac, flowering VERVAIN symbolizes enchantment and faithfulness, and is under the influence of the sign of Venus (whose spiritual domain is love). It was often used as a charm against enchantment, and as a love philtre, and if you bathe in water containing vervain you will be able to see into the future and every wish you make will be granted.

Who Will My Lover Be?

The APPLE is sacred to Venus, goddess of love, and has long been associated with love divination. Peel an apple in one long strip and throw it over the left shoulder. As it falls to the ground the initial of one's future husband's name is formed. Girls can use the pips, too, as a love oracle, pressing several to their cheeks, naming each one after a possible suitor. The pip that stays in place for longest indicates the future husband's identity.

But the apple also has associations with Pomona, Roman Goddess of fruit trees and one of the divinities of autumn, whose festival is probably what we now call Halloween. A girl wishing to know what her future husband will *look* like should take an apple and a burning candle into a dark room just before midnight on Halloween. Stand before a mirror and cut the apple into small pieces, throw one piece over your right shoulder, and eat the remainder whilst combing your hair. On no account should you look behind you, and as the clock strikes midnight his face will appear in the mirror.

An old country custom associated with the COWSLIP was to string up sixty or so of the flower-clusters, which were then carefully pressed together and tied to form a 'cucking ball'. Girls used the balls as a love oracle, throwing them from one to another, saying:

Titsy totsy, tell me true, Who shall I be married to.

The girls were picked in turn and the names of local bachelors called out. The last one to be mentioned before the ball was dropped would be the chosen girl's future husband.

At Michaelmas, 29 September, it is customary for girls to gather CRAB APPLES and arrange them in a loft to form the initials of their various boyfriends' names. The initial made from apples found to be still perfect on Old Michaelmas Day, 11 October, represents the strongest attachment and the best choice of husband.

The SNAIL was thought to have powers to foretell the future and one custom involved placing a snail in the fine white ash that dropped from the fire.

I seized the vermin, home I quickly sped, And on the hearth the milk-white embers spread.

The shape of the trail it made was said to be the initial of a future lover's name.

Slow crawled the snail, and if I right can spell, In the soft ashes, marked a curious L.

If you find an ash leaf or a four-leaved clover
You'll see your true love ere the day be over.

Young women wishing to discover the identity of their future spouse would place a two-leaf CLOVER in their shoes, saying:

A clover of two, a clover of two,
Put it in your right shoe.
The first young man you meet,
In field or lane or street,
You'll have him or one of his name.

If you dream of clover
prosperity,
love,
and happiness
are on their way.

A girl wishing to know the identity of her future husband should carry a sprig of IVY next to her heart on New Year's Day. She is destined to marry the first young man she speaks to. In the language of flowers ivy means 'marriage' or 'friendship'.

Girls wishing to *dream* of their future husbands should pin five BAY leaves to the four corners and the centre of a pillow before going to bed on St Valentine's Eve. Then, wearing a freshly washed nightgown, they should repeat the following rhyme before going to sleep:

Good Valentine, be kind to me,
In dreams let me my true love see.

The bay tree has romantic connotations. Apollo fell in love with Daphne, who had resolved to remain a virgin, so her father turned her into a bay tree to protect her from Apollo.

16

Good Valentine, be kind to me, In dreams let me my true

Variegated HOLLY was also used to induce dreams of a future husband or wife. Pick nine leaves on a Friday at midnight and place them carefully in a three-cornered handkerchief, concealing it under the pillow. The charm is only assured of success if absolute silence is maintained between the moment the leaves are gathered and the first light of dawn. Holly and ivy were used in fertility rites – the prickly holly representing the man and the entwining ivy the woman.

St Valentine himself was an early Christian priest, martyred in Rome in 269, but tradition has it that the birds paired on St Valentine's Day, so it seemed a suitable day to announce one's betrothal. However, the custom of sending cards and gifts probably dates from one of the pagan spring festivals associated with fertility or virginity, though in the past your 'valentine' would have been chosen by picking straws. Now it has become a way of discovering whether your love is, or could be, returned by someone else.

St Luke's Day (18 October) is another auspicious day for those wishing to dream of their future spouse. Although the patron of physicians, St Luke was regarded as a lucky saint for lovers, and in the past a physician might well have prescribed love potions. A popular love salve prepared for that day consisted of MARIGOLD, thyme, wormwood, marjoram, honey, and white vinegar. The marigold is the flower of the sun, which represents fertility. Their breasts, hips, and stomach were annointed with the ointment, whilst lying down on the bed and repeating the following lines three times:

St Luke, St Luke, be kind to me,
In dreams let me my true love see.

On St Agnes Eve, 21 January, the same dreams are induced by different means (St Agnes is the patron of young virgins). A young lover should take the pins out of a pincushion, one after the other. One pin is retained and stuck in a sleeve whilst saying the Lord's Prayer.

A sprig of ROSEMARY and a sixpence under the pillow have the same effect, or you can place a pair of shoes (which have been sprinkled with water) on either side of the bed, one containing a sprig of THYME and one a sprig of rosemary.

Another traditional custom on St Agnes Eve was the 'sowing' of BARLEY. The ceremony usually took place in an orchard, where the girl scattered the corn seeds under an apple tree, saying:

Barley, barley I sow thee
That my true love I may see,
Take thy rake and follow me.

Her future husband would appear behind her, raking up the seed.

On St Agnes Eve it was also customary for girls who were looking for a husband to make 'dumb' CAKE, consisting of eggs, flour and salt, mixed with water. For the charm to be successful the girls would fast all day, and then at midnight they would eat the cake saying the following rhyme:

Sweet Agnes work thy fast,
If ever I be to marry man
Or ever man to marry me,
I hope him this night to see.

Apparitions of their future husbands then appeared.

HERB PARIS is also known as True Love Knot. It is used in a rather complicated love divination ceremony, in which two girls sit in a room from midnight to one o'clock without speaking. During this time they pull out a hair for each year of their age, and place them on a linen cloth with the herb. After the clock has struck one, each hair is burnt separately, with the words:

I offer this my sacrifice,
  To him most precious in my eyes,
    I charge thee now come forth to me,
      That I this minute may thee see.

The future husband should appear, walk around the room, and then disappear, but neither girl should be able to see the other's vision.

LET HIM BE
DRAWN TO ME

Girls always ate HARE before visiting their sweethearts as it was said to make one beautiful for a week.

COWSLIPS can be used to remove spots or wrinkles. A herbalist of 1619 remarks: 'Of the juice or the water of the flowers of cowslips, divers Gentlewomen know how to cleanse the skin from spots . . . as also to take away the wrinkles thereof and cause the skin to become smooth and faire.'

The sparkling crystal drops which form on the leaves of LADY'S MANTLE were used as a cosmetic preparation for restoring female beauty, however faded.

For eternal beauty and youth, get up at dawn on May Day and roll naked in the DEW.

The spring-flowering LORDS AND LADIES is also known as wild arum or cuckoo pint. However, the phallic shape of the spadix gave rise to many ribald country names, and it is not surprising that the plant was used by young men as a love charm to attract the prettiest partner at a dance. The man would put the plant in his shoe with the words:

I place you in my shoe

Let all the girls be drawn to you.

MISTLETOE

The practice of kissing under the enables a young man to kiss his chosen girl without causing too much comment.

If a young woman has difficulty attracting the attention of the man she is in love with, she should hope to encourage him by walking barefoot at midnight in a patch of YARROW when the moon is full. With her eyes closed she should pick a bunch of the flowers and put them in a bedroom drawer or under the bed. At dawn, if the dew is still fresh, she will know that her love will soon pursue her. If the flowers are dry, she should try again at the next full moon or transfer her affections to another young man.

Once loved, yarrow could determine one's sweetheart's faithfulness. Herbalists used yarrow as a means of causing nosebleeds (which were thought to relieve headaches) by pushing the leaves up the nostrils. Subsequently this remedy was used as a means of discovering whether one was loved or not:

Green 'arrow, green 'arrow, you bears a white blow,
If my love loves me my nose will bleed now.

The country name for the ASH tree is Venus of the Woods and it has long associations in every culture with love divination and magic powers. An ash leaf with an even number of leaflets was used to find a suitable lover. A girl would wait with the leaf in her hand, ready to throw it towards a likely man as he walked by, saying:

This even-ash I double in three,
The first man I meet my true love shall be;
If he be married let him pass by,
But if he be single let him draw nigh.

A briefer alternative, without the guarantee that the right man was single, was:

The even-ash-leaf in my hand
The first I meet shall be my man.

THE LANGUAGE
OF FLOWERS

A charming medieval custom for a lady who was unsure of her feelings for her knight was for her to wreath DAISIES in her hair, which told him: 'I will think of it'. If she accepted him, she arranged to have daisies engraved on his shield, which proclaimed: 'I share your sentiments'.

In the Middle Ages ladies also gave their beloved knights sprigs of THYME as a farewell gift when they embarked on the long Crusades. A scarf embroidered with a design of thyme was also a favoured present. It meant 'loving remembrance'.

Shakespeare used the LANGUAGE OF FLOWERS in his plays, and most of his audience would have been familiar with the references and hidden meanings. In *A Midsummer Night's Dream*, Oberon describes where Titania sleeps, using flower symbolism to conjure up more than just a place of natural beauty:

I know a bank where the wild thyme blows,
Where oxslips and the nodding violet grows
Quite over-canopied with luscious woodbine,
With sweet musk-roses, and with eglantine:

Thyme symbolizes 'sweetness', oxslips (cowslips) suggest 'comeliness', a wild violet means 'love-in-idleness', the musk-rose represents love, and woodbine and eglantine mean 'united in love' or 'affection'.

The ROSE is dedicated to all the love goddesses and is a symbol of love and beauty. A red rose means 'I love you', but a yellow rose signifies infidelity and jealousy. A white rose symbolizes virginity, and rose buds suggest young and innocent love.

The flowers in a LOVE POSY can carry a message: 'Let the bonds of marriage unite us' would be made up with convolvulus, meaning 'bonds', ivy, for 'marriage', and a few straws, symbolizing 'unite us'; or a bouquet meaning 'Meet me tonight; do not forget', would consist of everlasting pea, for 'meet me', night convolvulus, indicating 'tonight', and forget-me-not, meaning 'do not forget'. If you present someone with a posy containing a red tulip, snowdrops, and heartsease, it could mean 'I declare my love, and live in hope; think of me'.

A young man should present a girl with a token of three ears of WHEAT as a means of expressing his feelings, but parental approval is necessary if the courtship is to proceed.

BIRCH is given by a girl to her young man as a sign of encouragement. If she wishes to discourage him she gives him a HAZEL twig.

29

HE LOVES ME,
HE LOVES ME NOT

To discover whether your lover is constant arrange some
APPLE pips on the grate of a fireplace with the words:

If you love me, bounce and fly,
If you hate me, lie and die.

If the pips burn noisily your lover   is faithful, but he is not
if they burn quietly away.

The PRIMROSE represents inconstancy, and lover's doubts
and fears, as the poem explains:

Ask me why this flower does show
So yellow-green, and sickly too?
Ask me why the stalk so weak,
And bending, (yet it doth break)?
I will answer, these discover
What fainting hopes are in a lover.

Sweethearts use it as a love oracle, too. 'Maidens as a true-
love in their bosoms place the primrose'. If it loses its
freshness a girl knows her lover is unfaithful.

The summer-flowering ORPINE, or livelong, is a useful oracle
for a girl who is courting. On Midsummer Eve she should
gather two orpine plants and set them on a wooden platter.
She can estimate her lover's fidelity from them – if the plants
flourish, all is well, but if they fade she can expect
heartache. The orpine's powers are referred to in
The Cottage Girl, published in 1756:

Oft on the shrub she cast her eye,
That spoke her true-love's secret sigh;
Or else, alas! too plainly told
Her true-love's faithless heart was cold.

An old country name for the DAISY
is 'measure of love' and it
is still the most popular gauge
of a lover's feelings. Pick off
the white petals of the flower
one by one, saying alternately,
'he loves me, he loves me not',
until the last petal reveals the truth.

A much more difficult way
of finding out the same
information is to turn a BLUEBELL flower
inside out without breaking it.
If you succeed your lover is faithful.

LOVE-IN-A-MIST is also known as fennel flower, love-in-a-puzzle, prick-my-nose and devil-in-a-bush. A girl who wishes her sweetheart to be faithful to her should grow this pretty plant in her garden. As long as she tends it carefully he will prove true, but should she fail to look after it he is likely to change. If through her neglect the flower dies, his love will die too.

In folklore the leaves of the POPPY are known as tell-tale leaves, for when they are crushed in the hand it is possible to discern from the sound whether one is loved or not.
If they crackle it is particularly hopeful.

33

An unchaste wife, or a girl of a flirtatious disposition, should avoid wearing PERIWINKLE in her buttonhole because if she is, it withers away very quickly and betrays her. (In fact, all should take warning as periwinkle droops very easily!)

Lovers used to keep one half of a LAUREL twig each in the belief that the other would remain faithful as long as they kept it. The leaf also has divination powers. If a boy writes the name of his girlfriend on the back of a laurel leaf with a pin, and the markings turn red after the leaf has been carried for a short time, the courtship will be successful.

The downy seed-head which the bright yellow DANDELION produces can also interpret a lover's feelings. Blow at it and if the seed flies off at one puff, the blower is loved passionately; a few seeds remaining indicate some unfaithfulness; many seeds, indifference.

To test the truth of a declaration of love in a LETTER you should fold it nine times and wear it all day, pinned near your heart. At night, place the letter in the left hand of a pair of gloves and sleep with it under your pillow. If you dream of gold and diamonds, or other precious gems, it signifies that your lover is truthful; if you dream of flowers he will prove false; and should you dream of white linen, he will die. But if you lose a love letter you may lose the love with it.

If twelve new PINS are thrown into the fire at midnight and the following lines are recited, a loved one who has been unfaithful or who has gone away will come back:

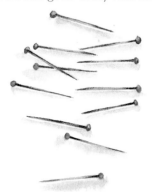

'Tis no these pins I wish to burn,
But . . .'s heart I wish to turn;
May he neither sleep nor rest
'Till he has granted my request.

TELL ME WHEN
I'LL WEDDED BE

Melt a small strip of LEAD in a teaspoon and drop it into a
bowl of cold water. The resulting shape will tell your future.
If it resembles a bouquet, a marriage will take place sooner
than anticipated; a tree predicts that you will live in the
country; a gun, that you will marry a soldier; and a cross,
that your future husband will be connected with the church.

A girl should pick some ST JOHN'S WORT on Midsummer
Eve, preferably with the dew still fresh on it. If it is found to
be thriving the following morning her chances of a good
marriage are very high. (The connection between the plant
and the date is that 24 June is the day of St John the
Baptist.)

The choice of the day on which to announce one's
engagement is particularly important. Preferably, it should
be at a time when the moon is waxing, although the ring
should first be put on the finger when the moon is full.

A young lady's future can be determined by the following old TICKLING rhyme:

If you're the lady I take you to be,
You will neither laugh nor smile when I tickle your knee.
Old maid, old maid, you'll surely be
If you laugh or smile when I tickle your knee.

Perhaps if you are unladylike enough to laugh, you will never make a good *wife!*

It is also possible to tell the future from a WILD PANSY as long as the flower has been given to, or picked by you, and not bought. The lines on the velvet petals should be carefully counted:

Four lines indicate your wish will come true;
Five, that there's trouble ahead, but you will overcome it;
Six, that a surprise is coming to you;
Seven, that you have a faithful sweetheart;
Eight, that your sweetheart may be fickle;
Nine, that you will go over the water to wed.

If the centre line is the longest, make certain you announce your engagement on a Sunday.

To discover who would be married next, several girls would meet in a barn, each hiding a ring under a small pile of corn. The COCKEREL would be brought in as the girls quietly watched, and whichever pile the bird selected first indicated a marriage for the owner of that ring.

Bishy, Bishy Barnabee,
Tell me when my wedding day will be;
If it be tomorrow day,
Take your wings and fly away,
Fly to the East, fly to the West,
Fly to him I love the best.

The LADYBIRD is said to have close associations with the Virgin Mary – 'Our Lady's Bird'. Other names include Bishy Bishy Barnaby (named after Bishop Barnabee), God's Little Cow and Cushcow Lady. If you find a ladybird you should place it on your hand, recite this old Sussex rhyme and then set the insect in flight with a single breath.

The first calls of the CUCKOO in Spring are supposed to reveal how soon a girl will be married. As soon as she hears the call she should kiss her hand to the bird and say:

Cuckoo free, in the tree,
Tell me when I'll wedded be.

The number of times she hears the bird after this indicates the number of years before the wedding will take place.

However, to hear the sweet voice of the NIGHTINGALE before the cuckoo is a very happy omen, signifying that your love affair will run smoothly. Should you be fortunate enough to be with your sweetheart at the time, clasp your hands together and stand in silence, mentally counting to thirty, and your love affair will end in marriage.

Those who are unsure how their love affair is progressing are advised to cut an APPLE in half and count the pips. An even number indicates an early marriage but if a pip has been cut through it foretells a quarrel with one's sweetheart.

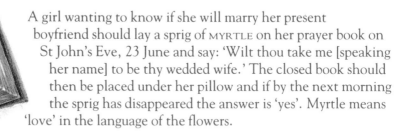

A girl wanting to know if she will marry her present boyfriend should lay a sprig of MYRTLE on her prayer book on St John's Eve, 23 June and say: 'Wilt thou take me [speaking her name] to be thy wedded wife.' The closed book should then be placed under her pillow and if by the next morning the sprig has disappeared the answer is 'yes'. Myrtle means 'love' in the language of the flowers.

on two eggs – one hatches out a male and the other a female, and they live together as mates for the rest of their lives.

A young man should carry a CORNFLOWER in his pocket and if it retains its colour he will marry his current sweetheart. Sadly, if the flower fades, she will marry someone else, as these lines from *Faust* suggest:

Now gentle flower, I pray thee tell
If my lover loves me, and loves me well,
So may the fall of the morning dew
Keep the sun from fading thy tender blue.

If a girl picks a handful of DAISIES with her eyes closed, the number of flowers she has grasped indicates the number of years that will elapse before she marries.

WEDDING BELLS

The DATE OF THE WEDDING should be chosen with great care because once it has been decided upon it is considered very unlucky to change it unless the circumstances are quite exceptional. A full moon is auspicious, and the following rhyme may be a helpful guide when choosing the day of the week:

Monday for health,
Tuesday for wealth,
Wednesday the best day of all,
Thursday for crosses,
Friday for losses,
Saturday no luck at all.

Lent weddings were generally considered unlucky.

If you marry in Lent,
You will live to repent.

Harvest time was even less acceptable:

They that wive between sickle and scythe,
Shall ne'er survive.

Every bride should wear:

Something old, something new,
Something borrowed, something blue.

Something old ensures that her friends will be faithful when they are needed, and something new brings success in her new life; something borrowed means that she may take with her the love of the family, and something blue is an emblem of constancy. But if a girl marries before her elder sisters they must wear green garters at the wedding. This may come from the custom in medieval England that part of the costume of an elder, unmarried sister at the wedding of a younger sister was green stockings.

When the bride is putting on her wedding dress she must make sure that all pins have been removed. A single PIN caught up in the folds will bring misfortune, whilst a small SPIDER discovered in the folds means she will never be poor.

It is unlucky for a bride to try on her WEDDING RING before the ceremony.

It is unlucky for the bridegroom to drop his hat on his wedding day, but a tiny horseshoe carried in his pocket will bring him luck. No telegrams should be handed to him on the way to church and money that he pays out during the course of the day must be in odd sums.

A tiny WREN singing in a hedge on the way to the wedding, is a lucky omen. However, if a bride hears a RAVEN croaking on her way to the church it means that, although she will have a large family, they will live in poverty.

ROSEMARY is the emblem of remembrance, and it also means fidelity in love.

Young men and maids do ready stand
With sweet Rosemary in their hand,
A perfect token of your virgin's life.
To wait upon you they intend
Unto the church to make an end,
And God make thee a joyful wedded wife.

On the appearance of the groom,
it was customary for the bridesmaid
to present him with a bunch of rosemary
bound with ribbons.

Rosemary also formed part of the bridal wreath which the bride took to her new home in remembrance of 'the dear old roof-tree which had sheltered her youth and of loving hearts that had cherished her'.

One of the bridesmaids would also plant a sprig from the bouquet in the garden of the bride's new home. In due course this would provide rosemary for the weddings of future daughters.

The decorative, tiered WEDDING CAKE of today, alleged by
some to have been created by a baker copying Wren's new
spire for St Bride's Church, bears little resemblance to 'bride'
cakes, thrown at a new bride as she entered her home in
Elizabethan times. But even then the baking was of
considerable importance to the future of the marriage:

Today, my Julia, thee must make
For mistress bride a wedding cake.
Kneade but the dow and it will be,
Turned to prosperitie by thee;
And now the paste of almonds fine,
Assures a broode of childer nine.

However, if the bride does not cut the wedding cake
she will be childless.

A DOVE,
the symbol of peace and gentleness, was often given
to the bridal pair as a wedding gift, with the promise of a
happy life. However it was considered very unlucky if the
donor had paid money for the birds, so something else was
usually offered in exchange for them.

HORSESHOES were originally used to protect newly weds from the devil's power. When the devil asked St Dunstan to shoe his single hoof, St Dunstan purposefully hurt him. In exchange for mercy the devil promised never to enter a place where a horseshoe is displayed.

Today they are still carried by the bride, and decorate the wedding cake and congratulatory cards. They are also thrown over the happy couple in the form of horseshoe-shaped confetti.

The custom of tying SHOES to the couple's car when they leave for their honeymoon probably has its origins in pagan times, when shoes were given as a sign of authority or good luck.

A weddin', a woo, a clog an' a shoe,
A pot full o' porridge an' away they go.

The prospective bride and groom should never have SURNAMES which begin with the same initial:

To change the name and not the letter,
Is a change for the worse and not for the better.

HAPPILY
EVER AFTER . . .

MYRTLE bushes, planted either side of the front door, ensure peace and love in the home.

A young couple should plant a patch of PERIWINKLES in the garden of their first home, to ensure a long and happy life together. The flower symbolizes 'happy recollections'.

SAGE symbolizes mutual love and domestic virtue and is said to flourish when the wife rules the household. As a result, husbands have been known to cut down a vigorously growing shrub for fear of being ridiculed by neighbours:

If the sage tree thrives and grows
The master's not master, and he knows.

Cybele, the mother of the gods, wore a crown of POPPIES, the numerous seeds being an emblem of fertility, and the poppy is dedicated to Ceres, Mother Earth, and Diana, goddess of love. However, it is also the emblem of Somnus, who represents sleep, and a potion of poppy seeds is more likely to induce sleep than fertility.

LADY'S MANTLE was known as a 'woman's best friend' because of its many uses. Distilled water from the plant is supposed to aid conception, and a decoction of the herb placed in the bath is thought to prevent any possible miscarriage. Then after the confinement it should be taken to restore the figure. HONEYSUCKLE, on the other hand, is recommended as a potion for 'hindering conception', despite the fact that it means 'we are united in love' in the language of the flowers.

If a pregnant woman stepped over a CYCLAMEN plant it would cause her to miscarry. Our ancestors took great care to prevent such a catastrophe and any cyclamen in the garden was covered with cloth if the lady of the house was pregnant.

To find out the sex of a baby before birth, suspend a gold wedding ring on a piece of cotton above the womb. If it moves in a circle the child will be a boy, if it swings backwards and forwards, a girl.

Monday's child is fair of face;
Tuesday's child is full of grace;
Wednesday's child is full of woe;
Thursday's child has far to go;
Friday's child is loving and giving;
Saturday's child works hard for its living;
But the child that is born on the Sabbath Day
Is bonny, blithe, good, and gay.

To prevent his wife from being unfaithful a man should take some hair from around the eyes and throat of a WOLF, together with a few whiskers, burn them, and place a pinch of the ash in a glass of wine.

GOOD FORTUNE

BEES are renowned for their wisdom and are considered lucky insects because they come from Paradise. If you have a romance that you wish to keep secret, be sure to tell the bees – and a hive nearby will make secrecy more assured. Bees also like to hear of engagements, weddings, births, and deaths, and to see a swarm of bees is a sign that good luck is on the way.

It is very lucky to give your sweetheart a black KITTEN, but unlucky to give her a DOG.

It is very unlucky to pick a PANSY sprinkled with dew drops as this will cause the death of a loved one.

ST JOHN'S WORT is believed to protect one against evil spirits:

St John's Wort, scaring from the midnight heath
The witch and goblin with its spicy breath.

A ROBIN singing on your window-sill foretells happiness in love and if the bird nests near a house it is a sign of good luck for the occupants.

The common PIN has always been an object of superstition, probably dating from the days when metal was in short supply:

See a pin and pick it up,
All the day you'll have good luck.
See a pin and let it lay,
And you'll rue it all the day.

Having a MOLE on your body is considered lucky. If it is above the right eye it indicates wealth and happiness in marriage, and above the left, a flirtatious disposition. A mole on the nose means success in business and one on either cheek foretells happiness generally. On the ear it is a sign of contentment, and one on the chin means you will be fortunate in choosing your friends. If it is on the neck you are a patient person, whilst one on the shoulders suggests fortitude of character and one on the hand means you can take care of yourself.

The MAGPIE is generally regarded as an uncanny bird and sightings of one or more magpies are held to be prophetic:

One for anger,

Two for mirth,

Four for a birth,

Six for gold,

Three for a wedding,

Five for silver,

Seven for a secret

Never to be told.

The smaller members of the SPIDER family have always been associated with luck and on no account should a spider found in the house be harmed – always place it safely out of doors.

The RAVEN is a bird of ill-omen, fabled to bring bad luck, foul weather and famine, or even death. In legend ravens were originally as white as Swans but it was a raven who told Apollo that the nymph with whom he was passionately in love was unfaithful. The god shot the nymph, Coronis, with his dart, but hated the bird for bringing bad tidings:

He blacked the raven o'er
And bid him prate in his white plumes no more.

The sight of CROWS, also considered unlucky, sitting on a path foretold the following, depending on their numbers:

One crow was bad luck,
Two crows good luck,
Three crows a wedding,
Four crows a burying,
Five crows speed,
Six crows very good luck indeed.